AF427055

JAMES

Faith that works

José Young

Ediciones Crecimiento Cristiano

Young, José

James : Faith that works / José Young. - 1a ed. - Villa Nueva : Crecimiento Cristiano, 2021.

44 p. ; 21 x 14 cm.

Traducción de: José Young.
ISBN 978-987-1219-50-6

1. Estudios Bíblicos. I. Young, José, trad. II. Título.
CDD 227.91

James is a translation of the study guide "Santiago" published by Ediciones Crecimiento Cristiano ISBN-13 978-950-9596-75-7.

1ª Edición inglés: Marzo 2021
ISBN: 978-987-1219-50-6

Córdoba 419 - Villa Nueva - Cba. - Argentina
+54 9 353 491-2450
+54 9 353 481-0724
oficina@edicionescc.com
www.edicionescc.com
Ediciones Crecimiento Cristiano
edicionescc

Index

Introduction

Studying James is not an easy experience. Not so much because it is hard to understand but because it is very demanding. James has no problem painting the situation in realistic terms and condemning certain attitudes in the churches. His letter reflects the stern words of our Lord against the Pharisees.

Despite it being a very old book, James is quite up-to-date and practical. The letter emphasizes problems and needs that we constantly see in our churches. Every church should study it as if it were directed directly to them, since they will surely see themselves reflected in the mirror that James offers.

One characteristic of James' letter is that he repeats key subjects several times. For example, instead of speaking about prayer in one place he touches on it in three different chapters. For that reason, we have divided the study into subjects and each lesson covers the parts of James that touch on that subject.

James

We encounter a variety of people named "James" in the New Testament, two of which are the best known. The first is the fisherman, son of Zebedee and brother of the apostle John. He was executed by Herod around the year 48 (Acts 12:1, 2), so it is very unlikely that he could be the author of this letter.

The second, that most commentators feel is the author of the letter, is James the brother of the Lord mentioned in Marcos 6:3.

It is clear that Jesus' brothers didn't trust him during his life but Acts 1:14 shows that after the resurrection their attitude changed. We do not have much information about this James, but we do know that he was one of the key men in the Jerusalem church, a "pillar" according to Galatians 2:9.

Since James was pastor of a church, we can understand why he chose some of the themes of this letter and why at times writes with very strong language. He knew the churches and could recognize their problems. They, like us, had the tendency to separate their faith from their lifestyle. But James insists that faith is something very practical, something to *live out*.

The readers

James does not directly name those who were to receive this letter. He speaks of the "twelve tribes in the Dispersion" but the majority of the commentators believe he is speaking in a figurative manner, and is referring to the many Christians (the new Israel, Galatians 6:16) spread throughout the Roman Empire because of the persecution described in Acts 8.

The purpose

In truth it would be more appropriate to talk about the purpose of the book at the end of the study instead of the beginning. That's when we can easily see the writer's goal.

Yet we propose James 1:27 as the verse that best summarizes the message of the book. In this verse James gives his definition of religion, and in one sense his book is a commentary and application of that definition.

"Religion" here does not refer to the content of our faith, to doctrine, but to its practice. It speaks of the external expression of faith, the way we communicate it and live it. That is the matter James deals with in this book.

Important note

To really benefit from James' book, you need to read it, and read it a lot. You should read it at least once before starting the first lesson. Look for another version of the Bible and read James there also. The more you read, the better it will become a part of your life.

We will refer to three possible versions of the Bible in this study:
RSV, the Revised Standard Version
NIV, the New International Version
ESV, the English Standard Version

1 Live the Word

James 1:16-18; 1:21-25; 2:10-13; 4:7-10

This lesson emphasizes something that is fundamental in all Bible study: our attitude towards the Word of God. The way we view the scriptures is a measure of the way we view God. We don't give the scriptures the importance they deserve because we don't give God that much importance in our lives. But for the disciple of Christ there is nothing more important than immersing ourselves in this book: it is life and light for us. But it is better if we let James speak.

James 1:16-18

In this passage James refers to God as light, as John did in 1 John 1:5. But in contrast to the strongest light we know, the sun, in this light there are no variations or shadows. And it is this God who does not change who gives us gifts.

1/Think for a moment. What are some of the gifts that God gives? There are many and not only spiritual gifts.

Also, by the will of God, we have been born anew. But the means of that birth, according to James, is the Word of God.

2/Can you find another passage in the New Testament
that affirms that we are born by the Word?

3/But how can the Bible be the means by which we are
born again? Don't we receive our new life through Christ
(John 14:6) and by the Spirit (John 3:6)? In what way are
we born anew by means of the Bible?

James 1:21-25

James explains here what we must do to make the Word useful
in our lives. "The perfect law, the law of liberty" that James cites
in verse 25 is the law of Christ, in contrast with the law of Moses.

4/In this passage there are at least five conditions we
should fulfill if we are to have a healthy Christian life
and not a mediocre one. What are they?

5/What is the situation of the believer who hears (or reads) the Word but does not apply it? In what way does he or she deceive themselves?

This passage explains why many "good believers" never advance in their Christian life. They appreciate the Word; they hear it preached and even read it. But the Word is not something we should just only hear, but also obey. We repeat: our attitude towards the Word is a good indication of the reality of our faith.

James 2:10-13

From all appearances Antonio is a good believer. He is faithful in attending church meetings and has a Sunday School class. He has a small store where he sells damaged merchandise that he received directly from the factory at a good price. He patches over the damage and sells the result at the normal price. His friend Paul commented to him about that practice but Antonio, angrily said: "What I do in my business is up to me. Don't try to bring the church into it."

6/How would you answer Antonio, according to this passage we are studying?

James 4:7-10

This passage hits pretty hard. We would feel a bit better if it were aimed at non-believers, but it is for us. How we should behave before God is clear:

- Submit (7)
- Draw near (8)
- Humble ourselves (10)

We put ourselves in his hands, we seek to know him better and we humble ourselves before him in gratitude and obedience. But there is a series of challenges to our lifestyle that are not that obvious.

7/For example:

a/ **What does it mean to "cleanse your hands" (verse 8)?**

b/ **Why should we mourn (verse 9)?**

c/ Do verses 9 and 10 mean that we should live gloomily? If not, how do we apply these verses?

8/As a summary, what do the verses in this lesson ask of us?

Conclusion

The verses we have studied in this lesson are a call to repentance, not to the sinners "outside", but for us. James attacks the cause of our spiritual weakness and explains the solution.

"But the one who looks into the perfect law, the law of liberty, and perseveres, being no hearer who forgets but a doer who acts, he will be blessed in his doing." (James 1:25 ESV)

2 Trials

James 1:2-4; 1:12-15; 5:7,8; 5:10,11

Problems, trials, and difficulties are inevitable in this world. Even though we now belong to the Kingdom of God, we share with all of humanity a world dominated by Satan.

We can, of course, suffer for the sake of Christ (2 Timothy 3:12), but we realize that the major part of our suffering has other causes. At times it's due to our own weakness or perversity. Other times it is the result of the injustice and sin of the people of this world. And we also share with all humanity the consequences of living in an unsettled world (earthquakes, floods, tornadoes, etc.) caused by sin (Romans 8:21,22).

In this lesson we will examine our attitude towards trials and suffering. What part does God play in all this? How should we react? What attitude should we take? Let's see what James has to say.

James 1:2-4

In verse 3 some versions have "steadfastness" and others "perseverance".

1/James says that when we go through troubles or are surrounded by problems, we should feel joy.
   a/ Explain why.

b/ If we don't feel it, what is the problem?

2/From your own experience, do trials always produce steadfastness? If not, explain what the reason could be.

The assurance that God can use trials and difficulties for our good is what helps us face them.

3/What is, exactly, the good that these problems should cause in our lives?

James 1:12-15

In this passage we will encounter two kinds of trials. One comes from the outside, and includes the normal problems we encounter in life. The other comes from the inside and it's what we call temptation. There is an important difference between the two, which we will explore in this section.

4/Is temptation a sin? Explain your answer.

5/Put the spiritual decline that James describes in verses 14 and 15 into your own words.

**6/When we realize that we are being tempted,
a/ what should we do?**

b/ what would be the result if we gave in to it?

It is important to note that James insists that temptation does not come from God (verse 13). If we fall, we cannot blame him; we are the responsible ones.

7/To conclude this passage, list the differences between a trial and a temptation (differences in their nature, consequences, our attitude, etc.)

James 5:7, 8, 10, 11

These verses speak again as to how we should face life's problems.

8/As a last question on this lesson, what are the differences between patience and passivity?

Problems can have two results in our lives, depending on how we face them.

- Positive. If they draw us nearer to God, if they stimulate us to seek him and know his will. They are one of the elements in the school of life, and are necessary if we are to arrive at spiritual maturity.
- Negative. If we turn inward, complaining and blaming God and everyone else for our problems, then the only thing we will gain is bitterness and frustration.

And, of course, the experience we gain when we face the problems of life with a correct attitude gives us the privilege of helping others in similar situations (2 Corinthians 1:4).

3 Prayer

James 1:5-8; 4:1-6; 5:12-18

In the previous lesson we emphasized the need to be a people of the book of God; in this lesson we emphasize the need to be a people of prayer. It's obvious that we cannot lead a true Christian life without prayer. The Word and prayer are the two links that tie us to God.

But when we get beyond the obvious, we realize that it's not an easy matter. God pays attention to our prayers, but there are also some clear limits. The New Testament outlines conditions we must fulfill if we expect to receive anything from God. The passages from this lesson explore some of those conditions.

James 1:5-8

1/According to these verses, what is one of the reasons why God at times does not answer our prayers?

2/Verse 8 mentions a person with a "double-mind". What would a "double-minded" person be like?

The expression "with no doubting" in verse 6 is key to our theme. It could possibly mean either of two things:

- Not to doubt that God will do exactly what we ask of him. In this case to have faith is to be sure that God will answer with just what we ask him.
- Not to doubt that God will do what is best for us. To have faith is trust in the goodness of him who will give us what is best for us, even if it is not exactly what we asked.

3/Explain why you think one of these two explanations is more correct that the other.

James 4:1-6

When we think through these verses, we can see that James offers three reasons why God at times does not answer our prayers.

4/Explain these reasons in your own words.
   a/

   b/

c/

5/James underlines the importance of our attitudes.
   a/ What is a "proud" person like? (verse 6)

   b/ How do you define a "humble" person? (verse 6)

   c/ What does it mean to be a "friend of the world" (verse 4)

We are not used to having people talk as bluntly as James does here, but we need it, since even among us there are strife, envy, friends of the world and proud people. According to James, it is clear why many times God does not answer us.

James 5:12-18

Verse 12 touches on a controversial subject, but it is indirectly related to the subject of this lesson. To "swear", in the Bible context, is to say something or deny something claiming God as a witness. It is as if we were to say: "I say this, and may God punish me if it isn't true or if I don't fulfill my word." To swear allegiance to the flag (which some object to) is a different sense of swearing.

James correctly says that the Christian has no need to swear that his word is true. What he or she says should always be true. There is no need to call on the witness of God to verify what he says.

Verses 14 and 15 describe a practice that most churches no longer follow.

6/Do you think that we should apply these verses? Explain why you are in agreement or not.

Verse 16 has nothing to do with confessing to a priest. It speaks of the relationship among brothers in Christ.

7/How should we apply the practice of "confessing your sins one to another"?

8/What do you think the benefit would be if we followed that practice?

Summary

9/Make a list of the reasons we have found in this lesson that explain why God many times does not answer our prayers.

10/What has been the most important part of this lesson for you?

4 The tongue

James 1:19, 20, 26; 3:1-12

One of the most common sins that is found in our churches is that of the tongue. Even though we generally do not consider it a sin, it is, and it does much damage. And we need to remember what the Lord said in Mathew 12:36:

"I tell you that on the day of judgment men will render account for every careless word they utter."

The matter is very serious for three reasons:

- the hurt we cause in others.
- the hurt we cause in ourselves (who trusts a gossip?).
- the Biblical warnings.

Of the New Testament writers James is the one who most directly attacks the problem.

James 1:19, 20, 26

1/How do you think we should apply the expression: **"Let every man be quick to hear, slow to speak."? Be practical.**

Verse 26 tells us how to distinguish between good and bad religion.

2/According to this verse, what is a "worthless" (ESV) or "vain" (RSV) religion?

James 3:1-12

James begins this passage with counsel for those who think they would like to be teachers.

3/Why would he give this warning? What is the real problem?

4/Explain in your own words the main idea of verses 3 to 5.

The language of verses 6 to 8 is blunt, but the illustrations James gives underlines the problem that he is fighting. It would be good to look at verse 6 in other versions of the Bible.

5/In the same way as question 4, explain the principle idea of verses 6 to 8.

6/Verse 8 says that no one can tame the tongue. If that is true, what is the problem?

Many of us know, from experience, that verse 9 is true. We have heard persons who are quite faithful to their churches make accusations, gossip, and even shout in anger against their brothers in Christ.

7/Can a real Christian act like that? If so, what is the issue?

The most dangerous sin is the one we do not recognize. And
it's for that reason that we have allowed the tongue to do so
much damage. The first step towards a solution of the tongue
problem is simply to recognize that it is sin and treat it as such.

> "If anyone thinks he is religious, and does not bridle his
> tongue but deceives his heart, this man's religion is vain."
> (James 1:26)

5 Faith and works

James 2:14-26

In these verses James deals with one of the fundamental truths of the Gospel: faith. That salvation comes through faith is one of the foundational facts of our preaching, yet many do not realize that there is more than one type of faith.

In this passage James distinguishes between two types of faith. The correct one, what God expects from us, and the other common one, which is not what God demands. Many people are confused about faith simply because they do not realize the difference.

1/How do you answer the question of verse 14? Why?

2/Can you give a Biblical proof, apart from what James says, for your answer to question 1?

3/What does it mean here when it speaks of "works"?

It is important to remember that "to have faith" and "to believe" are synonyms. They mean the same thing. So, when James says that the demons "believe" (verse 19) it means that they have faith.

4/If the demons have faith,
   a/ What is that faith? Try to define it.

   b/ Why then do the demons shudder if they have faith?

James says in verse 19 that that kind of faith is not bad, but it's inadequate. He even says that if a person has that faith they do well.

But the trouble is, when we speak of our neighbors, they don't have faith but credulity. They don't even have the "faith of demons" since the demons at least realize that our God is a God of "consuming fire" (Hebrews 12:29).

James offers us two historic examples of faith in action.

5/What does James want us to learn from the example of Abraham?

6/What should learn from the example of Rahab? You can see her story in Joshua 2:1-21.

There is another aspect of this theme that we should clarify. Normally when we think of faith and salvation, we cite Paul in Ephesians 2:8, 9. But apparently what James says in 2:24 contradicts Paul.

7/Explain why there is no contradiction between Paul and James.

This lesson is important because so many people around us have a dead faith. It is true that they accept - they believe - that Jesus is the Savior, but they do not realize that knowing is not sufficient. This also explains why many people who make a "profession of faith" do not continue with a true converted life; they have responded with a dead faith, not a live faith.

8/How can we apply James' advice to our daily life or to evangelism?

6 My brother

James 3:13-18; 4:11, 12; 5:9; 5:19,20

If we made a list of priorities for the church, first in line would be to love God with all our being. According to Jesus, this is the first commandment of all (Mark 12:29, 30).

In second place would be to love one another as brothers in Christ. In John 13:35 the Lord said clearly that love is the main evidence that we are disciples.

But if at the same time we made a list of the main problems in the churches we would have to put, at least in second place, our lack of love for one another. We should be the most loving people in the world but in reality, we can see too much gossip, anger, accusations, etc.

In this lesson we will try to define the problem, look at the causes and think through the solution. The problem is very related to what we saw in study number four.

James 4:11, 12 and 5:9

These three verses speak of a single problem in a number of different ways. "Speak evil", "grumble" (RSV); "judge" (ESV); "slander" (NIV).

1/Just what is James talking about here? List some examples from your own experience of what this means.

2/How do you explain James' argument against these practices?

If we think a bit, we realize that there are many reasons why we do not have a right to speak against our brothers and sisters in Christ.

3/Besides what James says, what other reasons can you think of?

James 3:13-18

This is a key passage since it not only describes the problem but also explains where it comes from. It would be good to read these verses in more than one version of the Bible to clarify some of the expressions used.

4/These verses speak of two kinds of wisdom. What is the essential difference between them?

5/How do you describe the wisdom that is not from above, that is not from heaven? How can we recognize it?

6/In summary, if brothers in Christ don't get along with each other, what is the true problem? (James gives a partial answer.)

What James says in these verses is very important. We are not wise because of what we know but as a fruit of what we are. The brother or sister in Christ who knows all kinds of doctrine but does not know how to love is spiritually sick. That person would not have God's wisdom since His wisdom teaches us to live a life like verse 17 describes.

James 5:19, 20

These last two verses introduce us to the final question in this lesson: What should we do when faced with the problem James describes?

These are the last verses of the book, but also the last application note on all James has been saying.

7/In the light of these verses and Galatians 6:1,
   a/ Who should do something?

   b/ How should they do it?

   c/ What should their purpose be in acting?

We would emphasize again the importance of this subject for the life of the church. Jesus didn't say that the world would recognize us as his disciples because we have good doctrine, but because we love one another. Doctrine is important, of course, but doctrine without love is something cold, rigid and at times dangerous. Many atrocities have been committed in the world in the name of doctrine.

May John 13:35 and James 3:17 be our banner.

7 Rich and poor

James 1:9-22; 2:1-9; 4:13-17; 5:1-6

We can talk of many subjects where biblical concepts offer a contrast with what the world around us believes, and this is a good example.

We are in a world where magazines, Internet and TV seduce us with their values. James insists on an extremely different concept. There cannot be a separation between our economic values and our spiritual life since both depend on the Lordship of Christ over us. What should the relationship be between my Christian faith, my work, and my possessions? James offers some basic suggestions towards an answer.

James 1:9-11

1/James here speaks of the "rich" and the "poor".
a/ What must we take into account to determine if a person is rich or poor? What is the real difference?

b/ A person owning the same material possessions would be rich if they lived in one place but poor in another. Why?

2/In general, according to James:
a/ What attitude should the rich believer have towards
him or herself?

b/ Why?

3/Also in general terms:
a/ What attitude should the poor believer have towards
him or herself?

b/ Why?

James 2:1-9

In the verses we just studied James deals with the personal
attitude we should have, whether we are rich or poor. Now he
touches on the discrimination that is at times found in churches
due to the economic status of the congregation.

4/James gives us at least four reasons why we should not differentiate between the rich and the poor people in the church. What are they?

5/The discrimination problem can be even broader.
a/ Besides economic motives, what other things can create discrimination among brothers in Christ? Give examples.

b/ Do we presently have discrimination in our churches? Explain your answer.

James 4:13-17

6/In this passage:
a/ What is the attitude that James condemns?

b/ Why is that attitude bad?

7/Does this passage imply that we should not plan for our future? Explain.

James 5:1-6

Again, we see James using strong language. He speaks of the rich but does not clarify if they would be believers or not. But does it really make much difference? Sadly, these words could easily apply to many who call themselves Christians.

8/According to these verses, there are two basic errors of the rich that James condemns. What are they?

9/Can you list examples how we ourselves could commit the same errors? (use practical examples from daily life.)

Conclusion

10/Taking into account what we have studied in these lessons:

a/ How do you see yourself: rich or poor? Why?

b/ What do you think is the most important lesson you have learned from studying all of James?

Conclusion

Though we feel that James 1:27 captures the true feel of this book, there are two other verses that also would be appropriate as a conclusion.

The first is James 1:26. It's very easy to deceive ourselves. We know what the Word says, and we feel that with that we are fulfilling what God wants. But if we do not obey what we know, we deceive ourselves. There is more than one gossip that has studied James, yet...

The second verse is James 4:17. We do not only sin by what we do, but also by what we do not do. Surely some of what James has said to you has hit very personally; may the Lord help you to be brave enough to live it.

How to use this study

These studies are study guides, that is, their purpose is to guide you in your personal study of the subject or book of the Bible that the guide develops.

What the study proposes is a discussion. We introduce the theme, suggest how to proceed with the investigation, we comment, but we also ask. The spaces after the questions are for you to write in your answers.

We are hoping that with this give and take we help you to build your own understanding of the material. Not second hand, as when you listen to a sermon, but as fruit of your own reading and investigation.

How to do the study?

1 – Before you start, pray. Ask God that he might speak to you and give you understanding during your study.

2 – When there is a Bible passage, read it more than one time and ask yourself: What is the writer trying to say? Even though many use the King James version of the Bible it would be good to have other versions available, so you can compare scripture with scripture. The Revised Standard Version, the New International Version or others can help you see the passage of scripture with more clarity.

3 – Do the lesson. Try your best to make as clear an answer as possible. Don't hurry just to finish. It is better to go carefully, thinking, asking, clarifying.

With the group

Personal study is important, but its value increases if it is accompanied with study in a group. A group of up to 8 people is ideal, but if the group is only you and one other person it is still better than studying alone.

Actually these studies have been designed with this purpose: to stimulate the study of the Bible in small groups. The system to use is simple:

1 – **Do one of the chapters on your own**. Even if there are things you don't understand, do your best to finish the chapter.

2 – **Meet with the group**. In the group you share the answers to each question. It is very possible that you will not all have the same answers, but then by comparing the results among the entire group you can clarify and if necessary correct your answer.

It is the discussion above all that provides the greatest benefit of this system of study.

3 – **Avoid getting off the subject**. It is easy to get distracted by personal issues or arguments about some particular question. If an important issue comes up you can dedicate a special session of the group to handle it.

4 – **Participate**. Everyone should take part. It is that which gives value to the study in group.

5 – **Listen**. We often have the tendency to jump in with our own conclusions before we allow the other person to finish. We will learn from each other, even from those, who in our opinion, are wrong.

6 – **Don't dominate the discussion**. It may be that you have the study down pat, yet it is important that you give space to others and encourage the possibly timid person to take part.

May the Lord help you in this task, and if you need help we are ready to assist you. Feel free to contact us.

OTHER TITLES IN ENGLISH

The gospel according to Mark: Who is this man?
José Young

This study guide deals with the central theme of the Christian message: the Gospel of Jesus Christ. The study is based on the Gospel of Mark, with emphasis on the person of Jesus Christ and our relationship with him.

Colossians: The visible God
José Young

Few of the letters in the New Testament emphasize theimportance of Jesus Christ as Lord as this letter. But Paul puts it in a realistic context, facing distortions of the faith that threaten to destroy the church. The best defense against error is a thorough understanding of the truth.To study Colossians is to get your teeth into the «meat» of the Word of God. There are some parts that are difficult to understand, but the effort to handle Paul's arguments is a rewarding experience.

The letters of John: In this we know love
José Young

The way God demostrated his love is very clear. It is he who took the initiative; it is he who sent Jesús to the cross to give us life.But what proofs do we have that we really love God? That is the question we will confront as we study John's letter.The message of John is so simple... simple yet difficult. The Christian life could be described by just one word: love. A word that's easy to say but difficult to live.

www.ingramcontent.com/pod-product-compliance
Lightning Source LLC
Chambersburg PA
CBHW072140150726
48002CB00004B/1566